Fox on the Wall

Written by Jill Eggleton
Illustrated by Paul Könye

Rabbit was hungry.
He went into
the garden.

"I will look for dinner,"
said Rabbit.
"I will look for a
big fat carrot!"

Fox was hungry.
"I will look for dinner,"
said Fox.

Fox went into
the garden.

Fox saw Rabbit
in the garden.

"A rabbit," said Fox.
"I like rabbits.
I like big fat rabbits."

Owl was in the tree.

Owl saw Fox
on the wall.
He saw Fox
looking at Rabbit.

Owl came down onto the wall.
Swoooooosh!

Fox saw **big** wings.

He saw **big** eyes.

He saw
a **big**, **big** beak!
"I'm going," said Fox.

Fox ran away.
But not Rabbit!
Rabbit got the
big fat carrot!

Labels

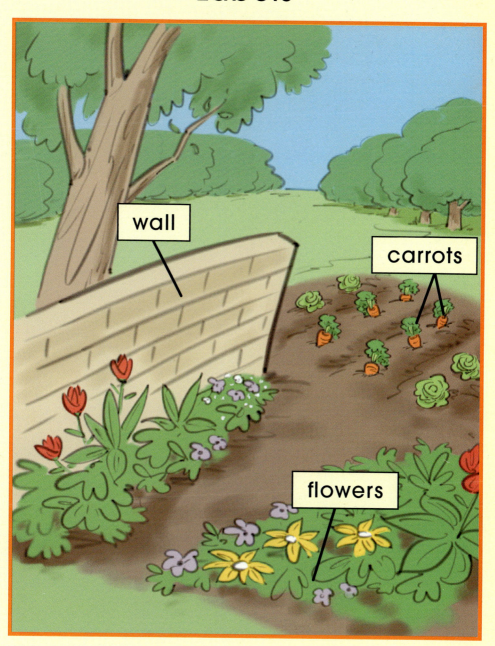

Guide Notes

Title: Fox on the Wall
Stage: Early (2) – Yellow

Genre: Fiction
Approach: Guided Reading
Processes: Thinking Critically, Exploring Language, Processing Information
Written and Visual Focus: Labels
Word Count: 110

THINKING CRITICALLY
(sample questions)
- What do you think this story could be about?
- Focus on the title and discuss.
- Why do you think Owl helped Rabbit?
- What else do you think Rabbit might have liked to eat from the garden?
- How do you think Fox felt when Owl swooshed down on him?
- What do you think Fox could eat?

EXPLORING LANGUAGE

Terminology
Title, cover, illustrations, author, illustrator

Vocabulary
Interest words: garden, swoosh, beak
High-frequency words: was, saw, came, away, I'm
Positional words: in, down, into, on

Print Conventions
Capital letter for sentence beginnings and names (**R**abbit, **F**ox, **O**wl), full stops, commas, quotation marks, exclamation marks